Seeing is Not Believing

By Jeffrey B. Fuerst

CELEBRATION PRESS

Pearson Learning Group

The following people from **Pearson Learning Group**
have contributed to the development of this product:

Joan Mazzeo, Jennifer Visco **Design** | **Editorial** Betsy Niles, Linette Mathewson
Christine Fleming **Marketing** | **Publishing Operations** Jennifer Van Der Heide
Production Laura Benford-Sullivan
Content Area Consultants Dr Amy Rabb-Liu and Dr Charles Liu

The following people from **DK** have
contributed to the development of this product:

Art Director Rachael Foster

Heidi Lane, Ross George **Design** | **Managing Editor** Scarlett O'Hara
Helen McFarland **Picture Research** | **Editorial** Nada Jolic
Richard Czapnik, Andy Smith **Cover Design** | **Production** Rosalind Holmes
David Glover **Consultant** | **DTP** David McDonald

Dorling Kindersley would like to thank: Andy Crawford for phototography, Carole Oliver and Catherine Goldsmith for additional design work, Johnny Pau for additional cover design work, and the model Elicia Oliver-Knox.

Picture Credits: Alamy Images: Imagestate/Pictor International 12. The Art Archive: Fine Art Museum Bilbao/Dagli Orti 19tl. Corbis: Terry W. Eggers 15tl; Julie Habel 22b; Joseph Sohm/Visions of America 18-19; Craig Tuttle 7; Stuart Westmorland 22t. ImageState/Pictor: Color Box 4. Masterfile UK: Graham French 28-29; Gail Mooney 14tr. Rex Features: Paul Brown 1. Science & Society Picture Library: 28l. Getty Images: Kaz Mori 16-17; Photodisc Green 27. Jacket: Masterfile UK: Gail Mooney front l.

All other images: DK Dorling Kindersley © 2005. For further information see www.dkimages.com

For information regarding licensing and permissions, write to Rights and Permissions Department, Pearson Learning Group, 299 Jefferson Road, Parsippany, NJ 07054 USA or to Rights and Permissions Department, DK Publishing, The Penguin Group (UK), 80 Strand, London WC2R ORL.

Lexile is a U.S. registered trademark of MetaMetrics, Inc. All rights reserved.

ISBN: 0-7652-5216-3

Color reproduction by Colourscan, Singapore
Printed and bound in China by Leo Paper Products Ltd.
1 2 3 4 5 6 7 8 9 10   08 07 06 05 04

1-800-321-3106
www.pearsonlearning.com

Contents

Exploring Light and Vision

Look around. Is sunlight streaming through a window? Does a lamp shine nearby? Light is an important part of our world. Can you imagine life without it? There would be no color. There would be no daytime. Without light, no one could see anything.

Without light, plants, humans, and many other animals could not survive.

The theory of light has been debated for centuries. Some scientists believed that light was made up of waves. Others believed it was made up of particles. Over time, scientists discovered that light has both waves and particles. Scientists study light and vision through the branch of science called optics.

You can see how light changes things if you shine a flashlight in a dark room. Rays of light will shoot out in straight lines from the flashlight. When the light strikes an object it can't pass through, such as a person's face, some of that light reflects, or bounces back, into your eyes. Your eyes then send a message to your brain. Your brain recognizes this particular set of reflected light rays as a friend's face. This is **vision**.

Now switch off the flashlight. The friend's face will seem to disappear into the blackness. Turn on the light again, and the face will reappear. Without at least some light, it is impossible to see an object.

You can change the look of a person's face by shining a flashlight on it in a dark room.

Rays of sunlight shine through gaps in the trees.
Light always travels in straight lines.

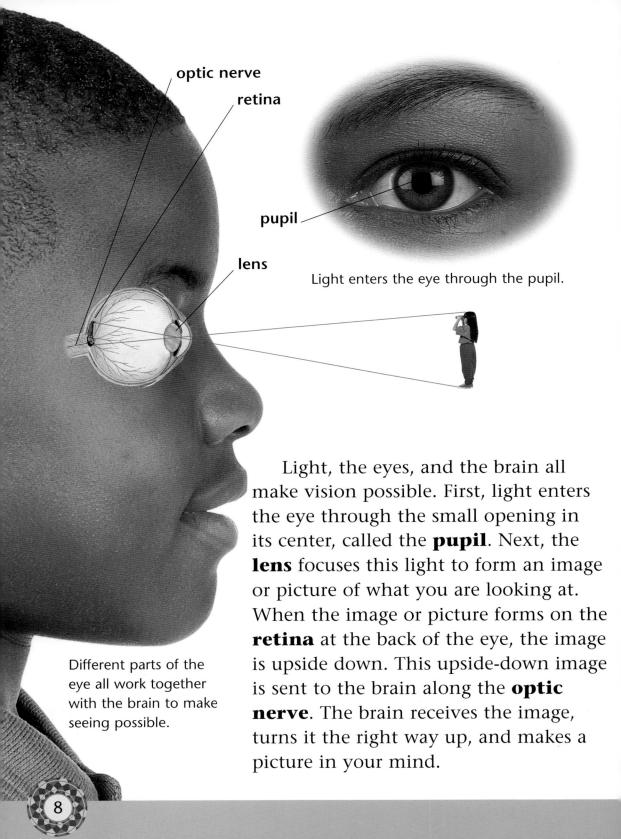

optic nerve

retina

pupil

lens

Light enters the eye through the pupil.

Different parts of the eye all work together with the brain to make seeing possible.

Light, the eyes, and the brain all make vision possible. First, light enters the eye through the small opening in its center, called the **pupil**. Next, the **lens** focuses this light to form an image or picture of what you are looking at. When the image or picture forms on the **retina** at the back of the eye, the image is upside down. This upside-down image is sent to the brain along the **optic nerve**. The brain receives the image, turns it the right way up, and makes a picture in your mind.

The eyes and brain function as a team. Since the eyes are set apart from each other, each eye sends a slightly different image to the brain. The brain puts the two images together into one. This ability is called binocular vision. It helps us judge distances and depth.

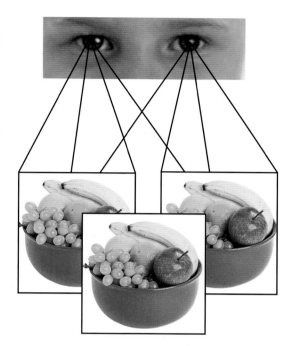

Your brain blends the images from each eye together.

See for Yourself: Trick of the Eye

1   Cover your right eye with your right hand.

2   Using your left hand, point to an object in the distance. Look at your finger and the object.

3   Continue to point at the object with your left hand. Uncover your right eye and cover your left eye with your right hand. Now look at your finger and the object with your right eye. Does the object appear to have moved?

Tricks of Light

When light hits an object, it can do many things. How light behaves affects what we see. Light can create dark shadows. It can bounce off an object and create a reflection. Light can also **refract**, or bend, when it moves from one material, such as air, into another material, such as water. Let's take a look at how some of these "tricks of light" work.

Shadows

A shadow is a dark area from which light has been blocked. You can explore shadows with a flashlight in a darkened room. Shine a flashlight at a wall. Then put a hand in front of the light. A shadow appears on the wall. An object that does not allow light through is said to be **opaque** (oh-PAYK). All that can be seen is the outline of the shape—in this case, a hand.

The hands blocking this light are making an animal shape. Can you guess what it is?

early morning Sun position

midday Sun position

late afternoon Sun position

The size and direction of shadows change during the day. The Sun appears to travel across the sky from east to west every day. As the Sun "moves," the angle from which its light comes also moves. The shadow is always on the opposite side of the object from the light. The shadow is longest when the Sun is lowest in the sky.

See for Yourself: Shadow Play

1. Place an object on a tabletop. Shine a flashlight on it.

2. Look at where the shadow appears. Notice its size and shape.

3. Move the flashlight from left to right. Now move it close to the object, and then farther away. When is the shadow longest? When is it shortest?

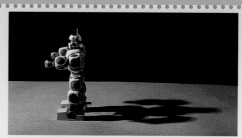

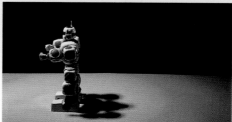

Reflections

Light travels along a straight path until something stops it. If the object that stops the light waves is smooth and shiny, it reflects the waves. It bounces the light waves back, like a ball bouncing off a wall.

Many flat, shiny surfaces reflect images, such as a pool of water at the beach.

See for Yourself: Light on a Flat Mirror

1 In a darkened room, shine a flashlight directly onto a mirror. Does the room brighten? If it does, it is because the light is reflected.

mirror

2 Now move the flashlight so it shines at an angle. Does the light reflect off the mirror? If it does, it reflects off the mirror in the opposite direction.

Your reflection from a flat surface, such as a mirror, looks almost identical to you. It is the same size and shape, but it appears reversed left to right and front to back. The person you see seems to have turned around to face you. When you raise your right hand, your reflection appears to raise his or her left hand.

When you look in a mirror, what is different about your reflection?

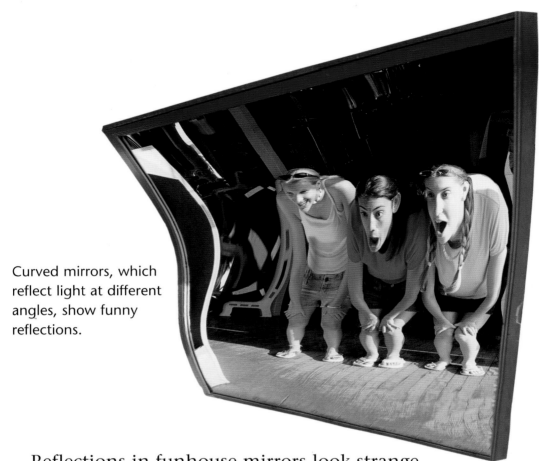

Curved mirrors, which reflect light at different angles, show funny reflections.

Reflections in funhouse mirrors look strange. Some images are stretched out, while others are squeezed and flattened. This happens because the mirrors are curved. These curved mirrors reflect light rays at many different angles, not evenly like a flat mirror.

A **convex** mirror curves outward and always makes objects appear smaller. A **concave** mirror curves inward. It makes objects near its surface appear larger and the right way up. However, distant objects appear smaller and upside down.

Convex mirrors, like this sideview mirror, make objects appear smaller.

Convex and concave mirrors have many everyday uses. The rearview mirror on the side of a car is slightly convex. It helps the driver see a wide view of the road behind the car. A makeup mirror is slightly concave. It makes the image larger. Curved mirrors are also used in telescopes and other scientific equipment.

See for Yourself: Convex or Concave?

1 Hold the back of a metal spoon in front of your face. The spoon curves outward like a convex mirror. What does your image look like?

2 Now turn the spoon around. The front of the spoon curves inward at the middle, like a concave mirror. Again, hold the spoon in front of your face. How does your image look different?

Rainbows

Have you ever noticed a rainbow arching across the sky following a rainstorm? Here's how it happens. Sunlight, which is actually white light, is made up of many different colors. When the sunlight passes through the tiny water droplets in the air, it's dispersed, or broken up, into light rays of different colors. These dispersed rays of light spread out into rainbow bands of color.

The colors of the rainbow make up the **visible spectrum**, which includes all the pure colors of light that people can see. Most people can see seven separate colors in a rainbow. These are red, orange, yellow, green, blue, indigo, and violet. Many other colors can be created by mixing together the rainbow colors.

See for Yourself: Colors in White Light

1 Cut a long vertical slit in a piece of cardboard. Tape the cardboard onto the outside of a glass filled with water.

cardboard with slit

white paper

2 Set the glass on a sheet of white paper so that sunlight shines through the slit into the water.

3 Look for a band of colors on the sheet of paper. These are all the colors that make up white light.

A rainbow is made up of many different colors.

Tricks of the Brain and Eyes

Our eyes and brain also affect what we see and how we see it. The eye and brain team gives us **perspective**. Perspective allows us to judge the size of objects, the distance between them, and their distance from us. For example, if you look down a long, straight road it seems to get narrower in the distance. The two sides appear to meet, although we know they don't. Artists call this the vanishing point.

When you look at this photograph, it appears as if the two sides of the road meet in the distance.

Artists use perspective all the time. Drawings and paintings are usually done on a flat surface. However, they appear to have depth.

Perspective is used in this painting to make the building look realistic. The more distant parts of the building appear smaller, as they would in real life.

Optical Illusions

People often use what they know to help them understand what they see. The eyes provide the information. The brain figures out what the information means.

Sometimes, though, the brain becomes confused by the information it receives from the eyes. This is called an **optical illusion**. Scientists study optical illusions to understand better how the brain and eyes work. Take a look, then another look, at some of these tricks of the brain and eyes on the following pages.

The arrangement of blue and black tricks the brain into seeing a woman's face or a man playing a saxophone.

How many legs does this elephant have? Not such an easy question, is it?

Do you see
a rabbit or
a duck?

In the pictures on this page, what do you see? In the optical illusion above, some people see a duck while others see a rabbit. In the illusion on the right, some people see a vase while others see two people looking at each other.

The image you see depends on what part of the picture you focus on. Once your brain knows the trick, your eyes will focus on one image and then the other. For example, focusing on the rabbit, without the duck popping into your vision, is now difficult.

Do you see a vase
or two faces?

What shape does your brain make from these clouds?

The brain tends to see things in simple patterns. It's constantly trying to make sense of the billions of pieces of information it takes in all the time. Much of that information comes in the form of visual images, which are stored in your memory.

Sometimes, your busy brain takes a shortcut. It guesses at what an unknown object could be, filling in details from its warehouse of knowledge to create something it recognizes. Use your memory of what a flying duck looks like to "see" this shape in the clouds, above.

What animal do you make out from the colored boxes above?

Your eyes and brain work together so that you see a heart, instead of six red shapes.

Your brain also gathers visual clues from its surroundings. Perspective helps your brain figure out how far away objects are. Your brain often compares the size of things with the size and shape of other objects nearby. However, such comparisons can be deceiving.

In the optical illusion below, one can appears smaller than the other. The key to the illusion is that the lines suggest perspective in the picture. Our brain tells us that the can on the left is farther away than the can on the right. Therefore, the can on the left seems smaller. In fact, the two cans are the exact same size.

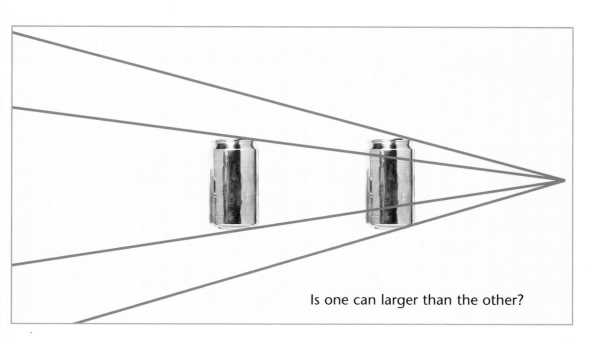

Is one can larger than the other?

What is around a shape can confuse us about its shape and size. Look at the crooked columns of white boxes below. The lines that separate the boxes seem to be tilting up and down. Yet if you trace any box, you will see that it is a square. This effect happens because the blue and white boxes don't line up. The illusion on this page occurs because your brain becomes confused by the information gathered by your eyes.

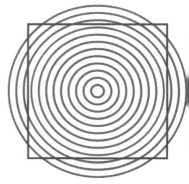

Are the sides of the box above straight? The lines seem to curve inwards, but they are actually straight.

Although the rows of boxes look uneven, the boxes are proper squares.

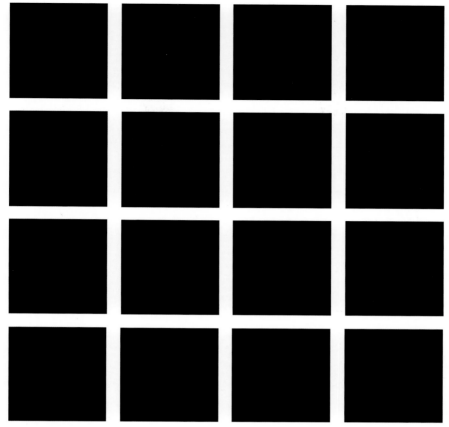

Hermann's Grid

Other optical illusions happen because your eyes can't gather all the information, or they gather too much information. The grid above is an example. It is an optical illusion called Hermann's Grid. Look at the entire grid for fifteen to thirty seconds. Do you see dark spots where the white lines cross?

This illusion occurs because your eyes see black squares and white lines. However, your eyes cannot process or send this information to the brain at the same time. So, the brain gets the information at different times. The result is the illusion of dark spots where the white lines cross.

Stare at the above image. Do the diamonds appear to be moving?

Some optical illusions seem to move magically before your eyes. Try taking the circles on the right for a spin. First, stare at the dot in the center. Then move your head toward and then away from the page. The circles will appear to rotate, or spin. When we change the distance of the circles from our eyes, the angled points on the circles become confusing. The brain tries to make sense of the confusing signals. It reports movement, even though the circles are not really moving.

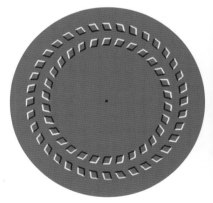

The circles appear to be moving.

Some optical illusions occur naturally in the world around us. One such illusion is a mirage. A mirage tricks the eye into seeing an object upside down or in a pool of water. A mirage occurs when a layer of warm air forms near the ground beneath a cooler layer of air. Light rays from distant objects refract, or bend, as they pass from cool air into warmer air. The light rays bend upward to our eyes and appear to be coming from the ground. Therefore, we sometimes see an upside-down version of the object. Look at the image below. It appears to be in a pool of water, which is in fact an image of the road.

Optical illusions found in nature are just as interesting as those that people make up.

Movie Magic

If we didn't know about light, shadows, and how our eyes play optic tricks, we'd be without one of the world's favorite illusions—movies. A movie only looks as if it's moving. It's really made up of thousands of still pictures. Each picture takes up a single frame of a very long strip of film. Each frame in a scene is only slightly different from the one before it.

When the film is passed through a projector, light passes through each frame. The picture is projected onto the screen. The projector lens magnifies the image.

Each movie is made up of thousands of separate pictures.

When we see the film, we never know that it is one picture after another. Our eyes see each picture for only an instant. Yet our brain puts the pictures together and sees them move. The brain's ability to do this is called **persistence of vision**. Before people invented the machinery to make movies, they entertained themselves with flip books. The pictures in these books appear to move because of persistence of vision.

See for Yourself: Make a Flip Book

1. Find or make a small notebook. On the first page, draw a simple stick figure with its right arm hanging down.

2. Draw the same stick figure on the following pages. Raise the arm slightly higher each time.

3. In the final drawing, the arm should be above the shoulder, as if waving hello.

4. Quickly flip through the pages with your thumb and watch your stick figure move.

Light, the eyes, and the brain team up to help us see and understand the world. They can also do surprising and unusual things—even trick us. By studying these tricks of the eyes, brain, and light, scientists learn more about how the brain and eyes work. There is still much more for us to learn if we keep our eyes and minds open.

When a person spins a **zoetrope**, the sequence of pictures will look as if they are moving.

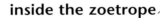

inside the zoetrope

Glossary

concave	a lens or mirror that curves inward
convex	a lens or mirror that curves outward
lens	the clear part of the eye that focuses light rays on the retina
opaque	a material that does not allow light to pass through it
optical illusion	a "trick" of the eyes and brain
optic nerve	the nerve that sends signals to the brain about the image formed on the retina
persistence of vision	when the brain remembers an image for longer than the eyes see it
perspective	the ability to use visual clues to judge the distance and position of objects
pupil	the opening in the center of the eye
refract	bend, as when light rays are bent by a crystal or water
retina	the back part of the eye, made up of special cells that react to light
visible spectrum	the colors that can be detected by the human eye
vision	the act or power of seeing
zoetrope	an optical toy invented in the 1800s; when spun, a sequence of pictures will appear to move

Index

Look at the circles in the middle of these flowers. Are they the same size? Measure the circles with a ruler.